WHAT IF HIGGINS HAD GIVEN UP?

The Story of the WWII D-Day Boats

WRITTEN BY:
CATHY WERLING

ILLUSTRATED BY:
MAGGIE RAGUSE

PUBLISHED BY:

Lowell Milken Center
FOR *Unsung Heroes*

To give up is to never know what you can achieve.

Cathy Werling

Carruth Higgins and his brother, Walker, stared at the raft that was slowly sinking into the pond. Grabbing the attached rope, they pulled the raft out of the water and sat on the ground next to it. Feeling very disappointed, Carruth looked at Walker and said, "That's it! Forget this! We will never get this thing to float!"

"Let's just go home and leave this piece of junk here," Walker said, as he and Carruth stood up, ready to head home.

Turning around, they were surprised to see their father, Skipper Higgins, heading toward them. He had overheard them talking and asked what was going on. As they told him about the hours they had spent trying to build a raft that would float on the pond, he could see how upset they were that it didn't work.

JUNE 6
1944
D-DAY

Skipper motioned for his sons to sit on the grassy hill next to the pond, as he asked, "Boys, do you know anything about Great-Grandfather Higgins?"

"Well," said Walker, "His name was Andrew Jackson Higgins, and he had something to do with D-Day."

"Yes," Carruth added, "people say his D-Day boats helped the United States win a war."

Skipper replied, "Those facts are true, but what he did was no easy thing and certainly didn't succeed at first! In fact, many of his life's plans took several tries."

"When your great-grandpa was only nine, he learned to work hard, not giving up when things didn't go his way. Because his father had died, it became important for Andrew to help make money for his family. He began cutting grass for people, using only a hand-tool called a sickle."

"After earning enough money, he bought a lawn mower so he could cut grass more quickly. Not wanting to lose customers, Andrew grew his business until he owned seventeen mowers. He hired older, stronger boys to do the mowing, while he organized the jobs and schedules."

"At the age of twelve, your great-grandfather worked at delivering newspapers for The Omaha Daily News. He set up delivery routes, sold the newspaper subscriptions, and collected the payments. He hired others to actually deliver the papers, while still making it possible to earn $100 for himself. After one year, he was able to sell his business to an adult for $1,700."

"Also, when he was twelve, Andrew was set on having his own boat, one he hoped would have lots of speed. He found a wrecked sailboat at a lake near his home. He worked hard to repair it, naming it Patience because working on it was not an easy job! After much hard work to make Patience like new, the boat was just too slow for his liking."

"Still working to have a fast boat, Andrew decided to build his own iceboat, which he did in his family's basement. All went well with the boat he named The Annie'O, until he discovered he could not get it out of the basement."

"While others would have given up, he did not! With borrowed equipment, Andrew and his friends took bricks out of the basement wall, moved the boat outside, rebuilt the wall of bricks, and got The Annie'O on a frozen lake. The boat glided across that lake at a speed near sixty miles an hour, just like he had hoped."

"That's not to say everything always went right for your great-grandpa. When he was in high school, he made some poor choices and did not always do things as his teachers expected. Rather than stay in school until graduation, he left school after his junior year and joined the National Guard. His love of boats grew even stronger when he and his fellow soldiers used pontoon boats to create a bridge for crossing the Platte River."

"After two summers of experience as a logger in Wyoming, 20-year-old Andrew found a new interest in working with lumber. He moved to Alabama, where he used his savings to buy a farm with many acres of timber land. During those early days in Alabama, he learned all he could about the lumber business, met and married his wife, Angele, and opened his own sawmill."

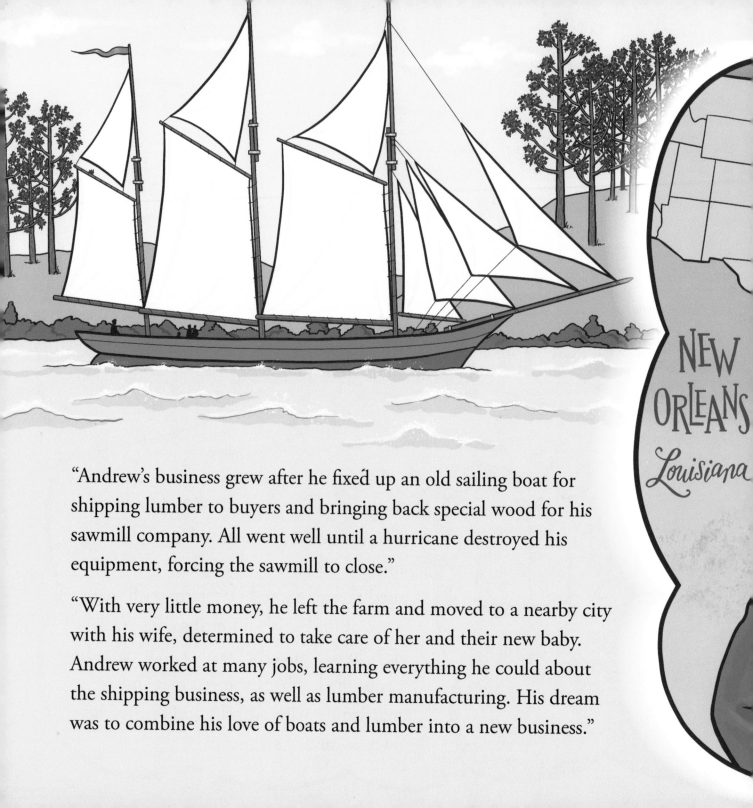

NEW
ORLEANS
Louisiana

"Andrew's business grew after he fixed up an old sailing boat for shipping lumber to buyers and bringing back special wood for his sawmill company. All went well until a hurricane destroyed his equipment, forcing the sawmill to close."

"With very little money, he left the farm and moved to a nearby city with his wife, determined to take care of her and their new baby. Andrew worked at many jobs, learning everything he could about the shipping business, as well as lumber manufacturing. His dream was to combine his love of boats and lumber into a new business."

A.J. HIGGINS
LUMBER & EXPORT

"With much hard work and a 'never-give-up' attitude, Andrew's dream became real, when at the age of 26, he and his family moved to New Orleans, where he worked for a lumber company. That job gave Andrew the chance to start his own business, A.J. Higgins Lumber and Export Company."

"During that time, your great-grandfather bought cheap timberland in Mississippi where shallow water made it hard to get logs out on rafts. Boats with enough power had trouble in the shallow water, and boats that traveled well in shallow water didn't have enough power."

"To fix this problem, he created a tunnel boat, on which a powerful propeller was placed in a hump or 'tunnel' that protected it from objects in the shallow water. The strong propeller gave the boat power to haul the logs, while the boat's flatter bottom helped it move easily in shallow water."

EUREKA

Tunnel Boat

"As his boat design became more widely known and popular, boatbuilding became Andrew's main business. Many companies, even the U.S. Coast Guard, used these small, smooth, and fast Higgins' boats, which he named Eureka Boats."

"While Andrew's business grew, the United States faced the threat of war and needed to have a well-prepared military for defending U.S. freedom. Your great-grandpa believed his Eureka Boats were needed in the event of war. For years, he worked to convince the Navy how valuable they could be."

"Refusing to give up, he was finally allowed to submit the Eureka Boat for a test. It performed much better than other boats, and the Higgins' company was asked to produce boats for the Navy. Andrew continued working to improve his boats so they could best meet the Navy's needs."

"Once World War II began and the U.S. entered the war, there was a great need for Higgins' special boats. Because of this, Andrew Higgins' boat company grew quickly from one small warehouse with around 50 workers to a company that had eight city plants which produced over 20,000 boats. In these plants, Higgins paid equal wages to over 20,000 hard-working men and women of many races."

LCVP
boats

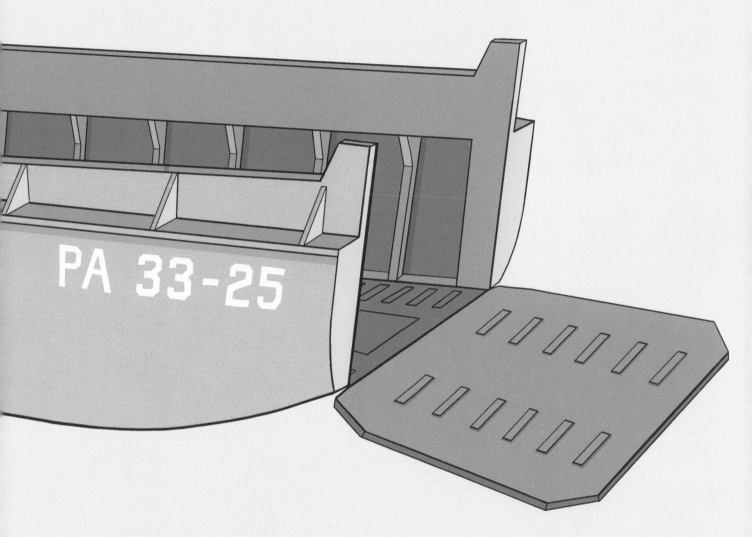

PA 33-25

"Of all the boats designed and produced by Andrew, the most famous were his LCVPs (Landing Craft, Vehicle, Personnel), better known as the Higgins Boats. They were based on the Eureka Boats, with the propeller tunnels and flatter bottoms, but had an added pull-down ramp which allowed for quick and easy unloading of soldiers and equipment. Each boat could hold 36 men and a jeep or 12 men and 8,000 pounds of supplies."

"These were the boats used on an important mission that helped to end World War II and defeat the enemy. Thousands of the Higgins Boats were loaded with troops and supplies. They were sent secretly to land on the beaches of Normandy, France for a surprise attack on the enemy. Because the boats were able to travel in very shallow water, they could land right on the sandy beaches far away from the docks at big city ports."

NORMANDY, France

D-DAY

"The day of this mission, called D-Day, led to the defeat of those countries who had planned to 'rule the world.' The Higgins Boats were used in many important missions throughout the Pacific Ocean, as well. President Eisenhower even said, 'Andrew Higgins is the man who won the war for us.' Though we know he was just part of what it took to win the war, his was a very important part!"

"So, boys, you see that Great-Grandfather Higgins had many choices during his life, and there were often times he could have given up when things did not go his way. However, he was always determined to reach his goals, and giving up was never a choice for him!"

"Wow!" said Walker. "Thanks for sharing that story, Dad. I had no idea of all our great-grandpa had done."

"I think I've learned something from him," added Carruth. "I see that nothing he did would have happened if he'd quit when things got hard."

Both boys looked at each other and then at their raft lying near the water. As they got up and headed back to work, they were ready to do whatever it would take to get their project completed.

Learning about Andrew Jackson Higgins: Author's Sources

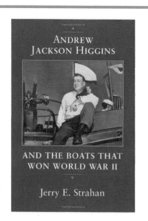

Many of the amazing stories about Andrew Jackson Higgins' determined approach to life came from Jerry Strahan, the author of *Andrew Jackson Higgins and the Boats That Won World War II*. In personal conversations with Jerry and through reading his book, much was learned about the many hours of interviews and personal research he had done. He uncovered much information about AJH by talking to family members and people who had worked for Higgins. His book provides detailed information about each step in Andrew's life that led to the development of his famous Higgins Boats. He also shares many photos of Higgins and of his many companies and boats.

More information about Higgins was gained from Jerry Meyer, who along with his students at Columbus High School, conceived, designed, and completed The Andrew Jackson Higgins National Memorial in Columbus, Nebraska, which is the birthplace of Mr. Higgins. Central to the Higgins Memorial Project is a life-sized replica of an LCVP "Higgins Boat", which is set in sand, as if on a beach. Visitors can walk inside by going up the lowered ramp. The sand surrounding the boat is mixed with samples of sand collected from many of the invasion beaches of WWII, Korea, and Vietnam.

Skipper Higgins, one of the grandsons of Andrew Jackson Higgins, shared family stories that had been preserved and passed down about his grandfather. Stories Skipper told about two of his own sons, Carruth and Walker, sparked the idea for sharing the influence and positive example of Andrew Higgins on future generations of his own family. That same positive, "never-give-up" attitude can be a powerful role model for all who learn his story.

THE AUTHOR

Cathy Werling is an award-winning elementary educator living in Fort Scott, Kansas. Her passion for helping students develop positive character traits and seek out worthy role models led to her part time work at the Lowell Milken Center for Unsung Heroes. *What If Higgins Had Given Up?* is the fourth book in her series of children's books about special unsung heroes whose lives can be worthy examples for children. By sharing the story of Andrew Jackson Higgins, Cathy helps them learn the importance of perseverance and determination in reaching their goals, even when facing obstacles.

THE ILLUSTRATOR

Maggie Raguse, owner of Raguse Creative Services in Portland, Oregon, has been a prolific illustrator and graphic designer for over three decades. She specializes in fashion illustration and surface design and has a warm place in her heart for illustrating children's books. Collaborating with Cathy Werling in supporting the mission of the Lowell Milken Center for Unsung Heroes has been a rich and rewarding experience for her.

CPSIA information can be obtained
at www.ICGtesting.com
Printed in the USA
LVHW011119080421
683781LV00002B/18